COMPOSER SHOWCASE
HAL LEONARD
STUDENT PIANO LIBRARY

Fanciful Waltzes

FIVE CHARACTER PIECES FOR PIANO SOLO

BY CAROL KLOSE

CONTENTS

Edited by J. Mark Baker

ISBN 0-634-07440-7

HAL•LEONARD®
CORPORATION
7777 W. BLUEMOUND RD. P.O. BOX 13819 MILWAUKEE, WI 53213

In Australia Contact:
Hal Leonard Australia Pty. Ltd.
22 Taunton Drive P.O. Box 5130
Cheltenham East, 3192 Victoria, Australia
Email: ausadmin@halleonard.com

Visit Hal Leonard Online at
www.halleonard.com

Crystal Ballerina

Carol Klose

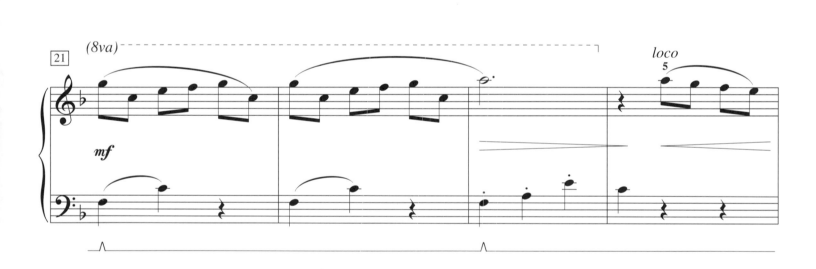

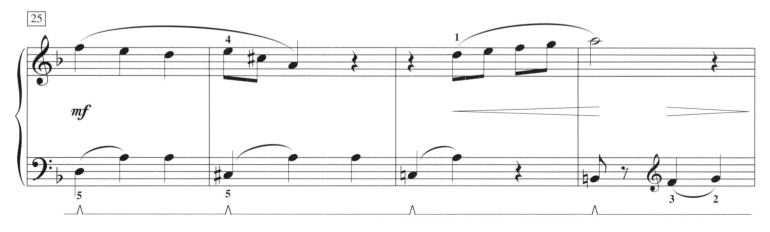

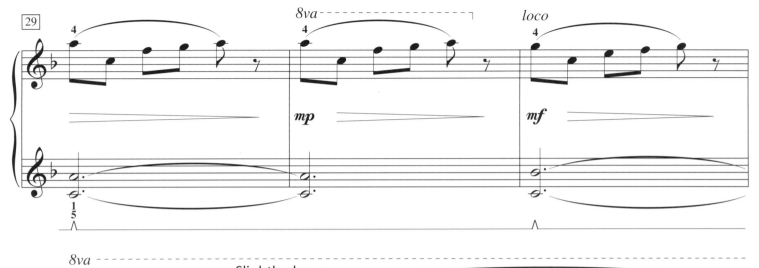

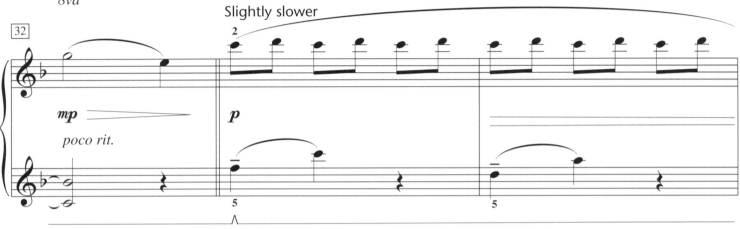

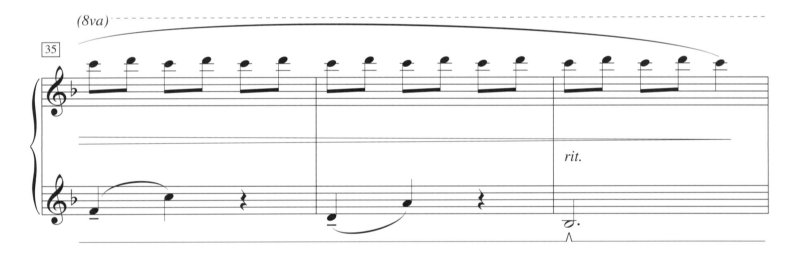

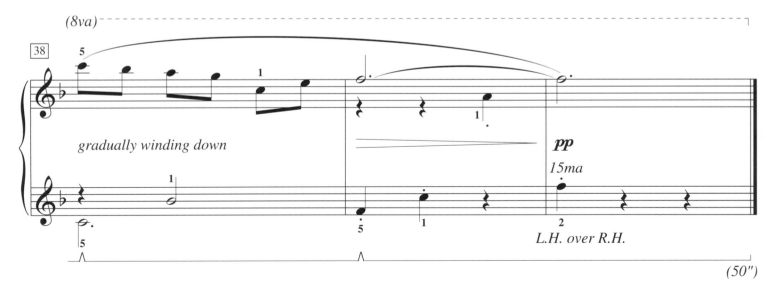

(50")

Transylvania Ball

Carol Klose

Eerily bright Waltz tempo ($\, \bullet \,$ = 168–184)

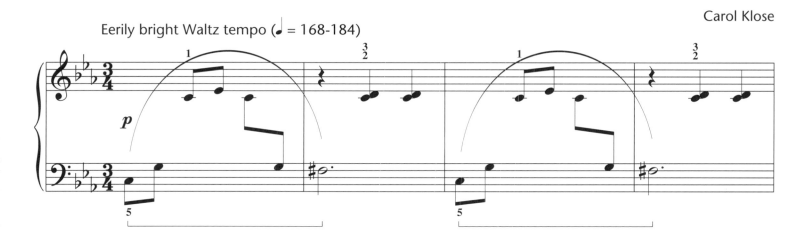

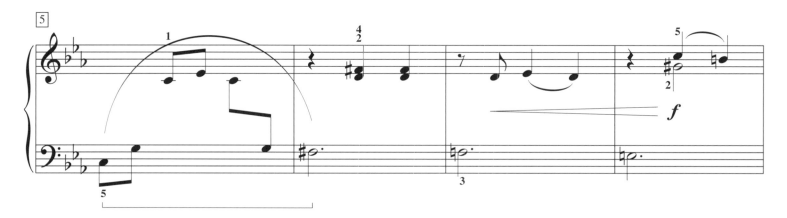

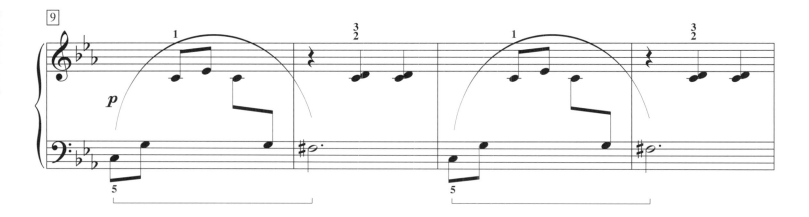

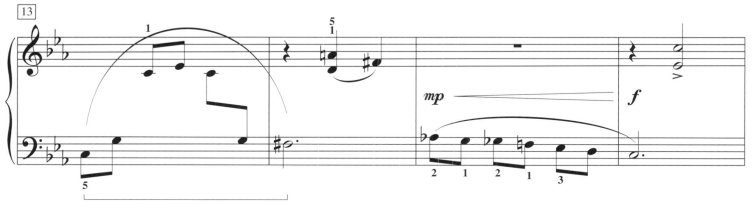

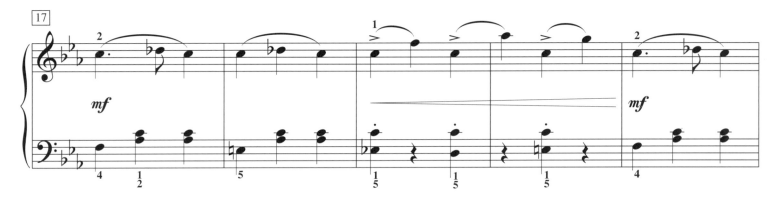

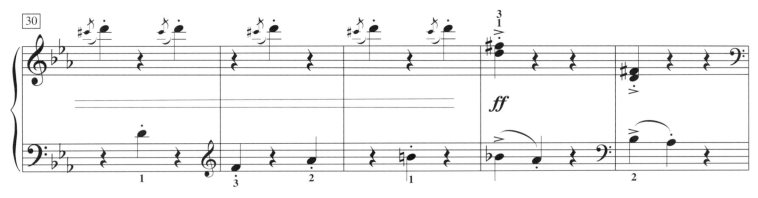

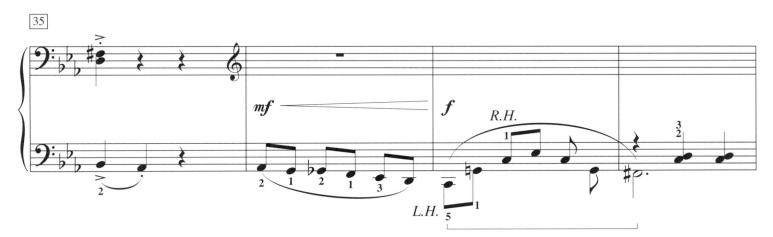

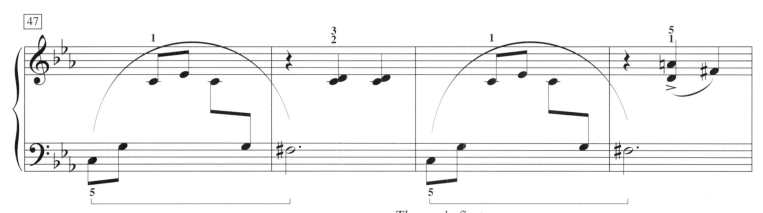

The sun's first rays

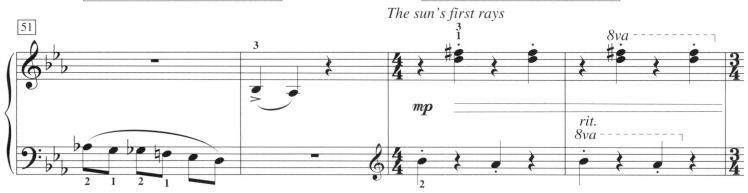

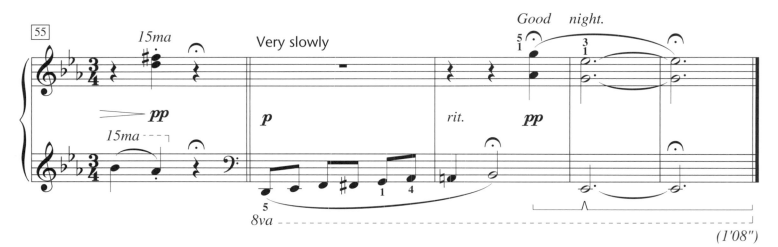

Good   night.

Very slowly

(1'08")

7

Lullaby In Blue

Carol Klose

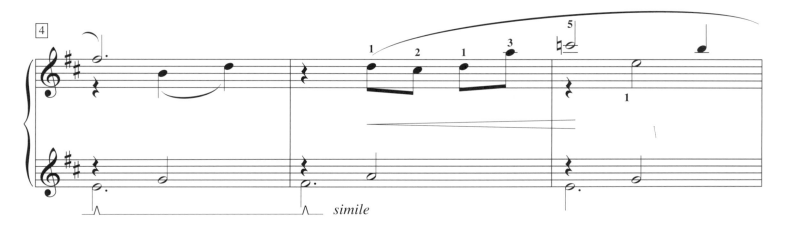

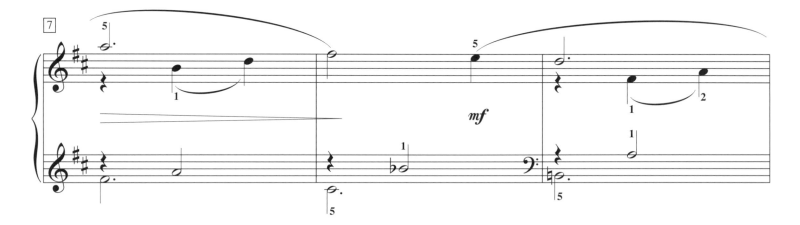

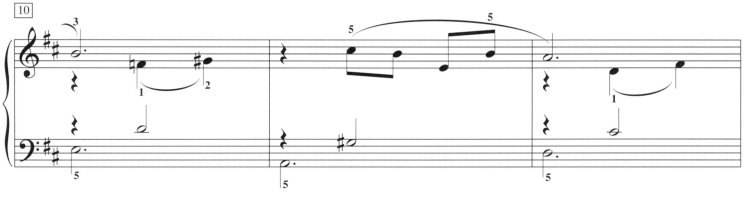

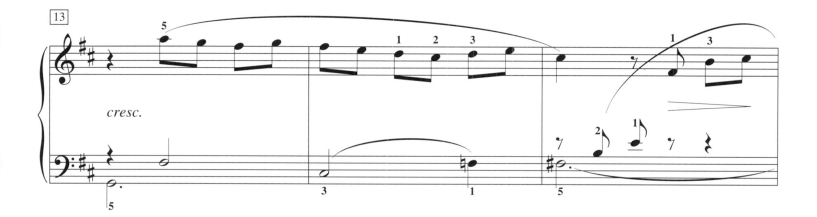

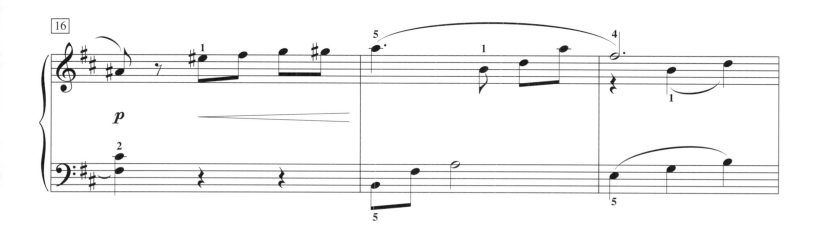

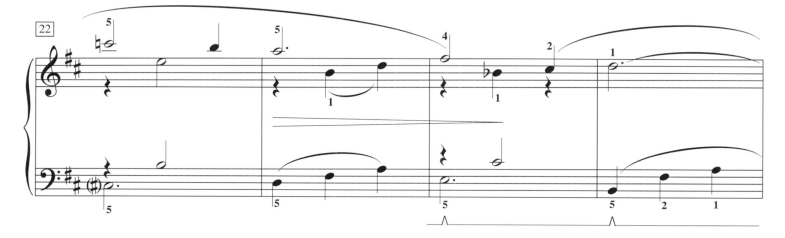

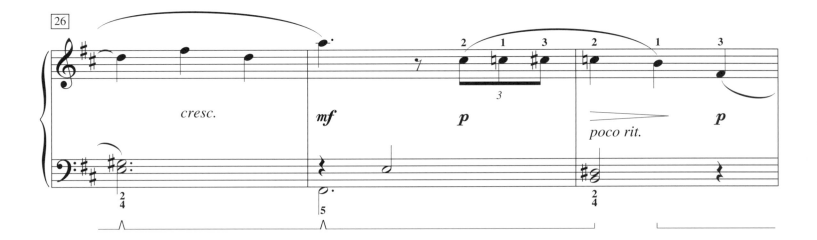

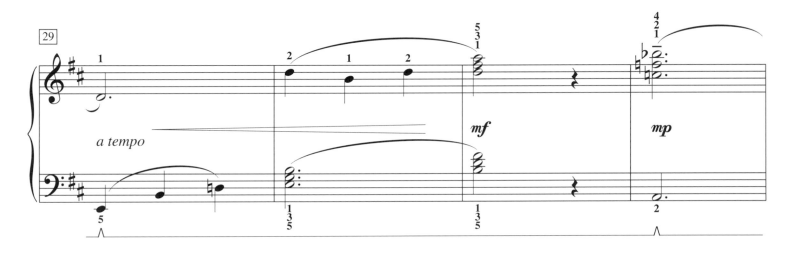

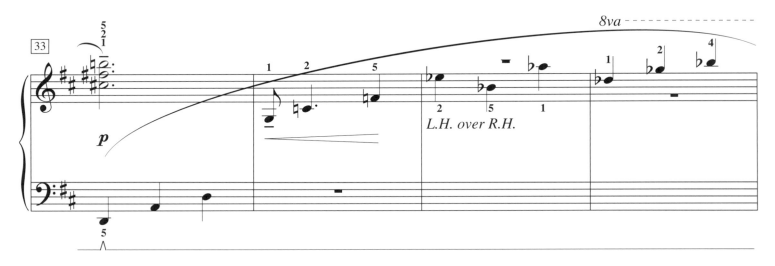

(1'06")

Petite Waltz

Carol Klose

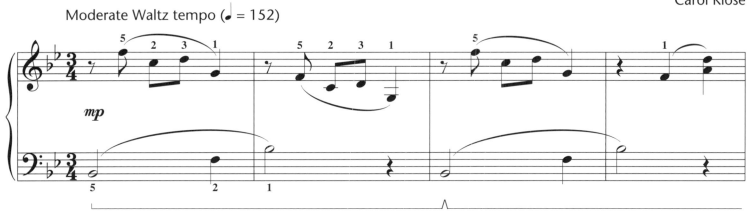

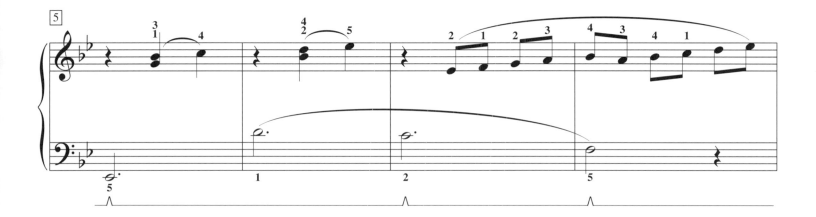

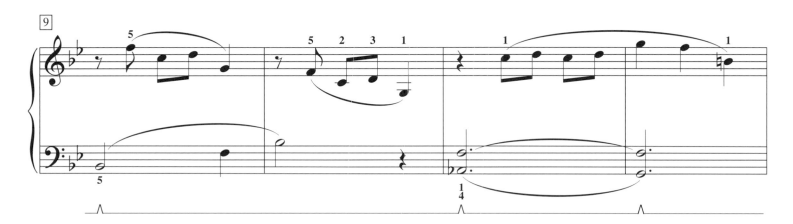

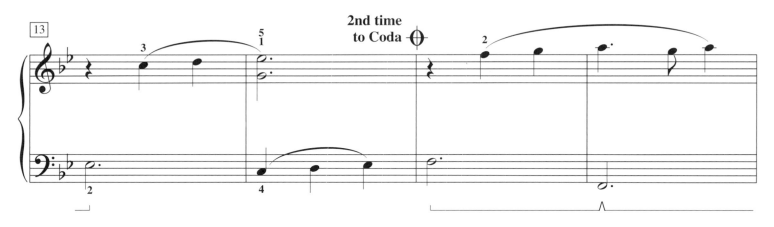

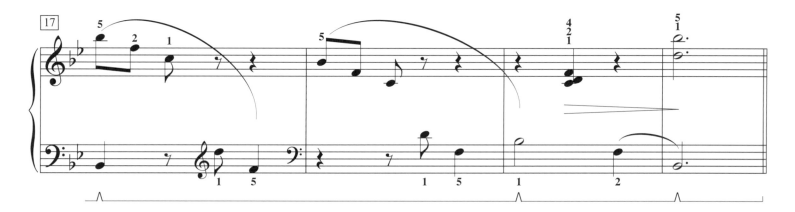

Più mosso (♩ = 168-176)

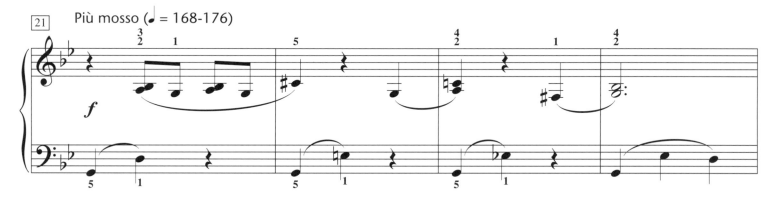

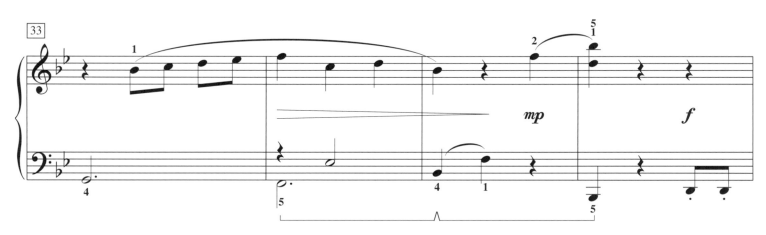

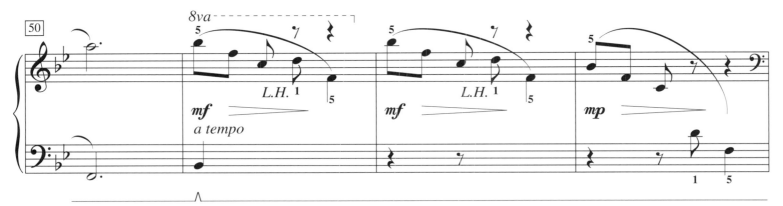

(1'30")

Maestro, There's A Fly In My Waltz

Carol Klose

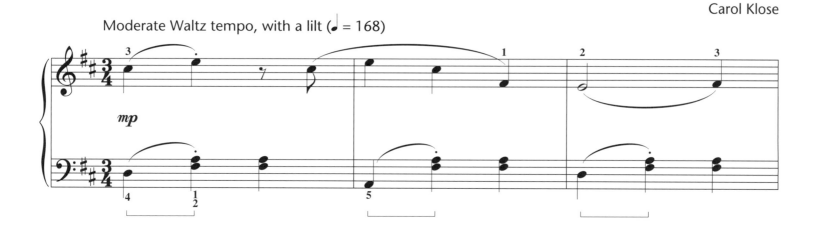

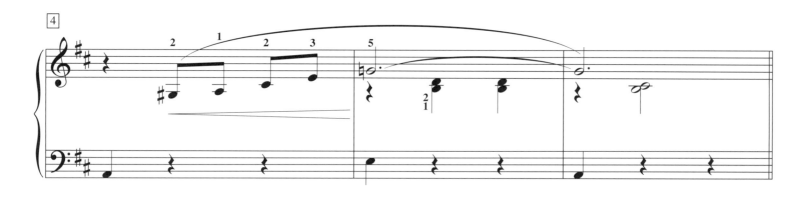

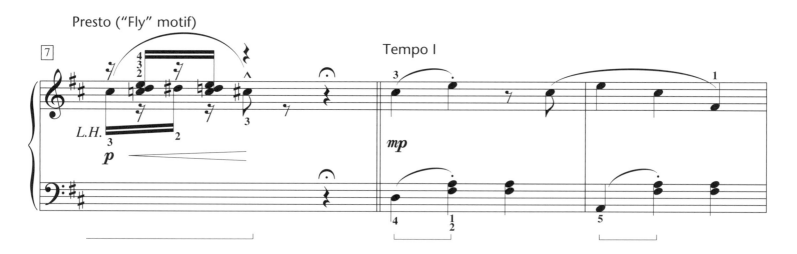

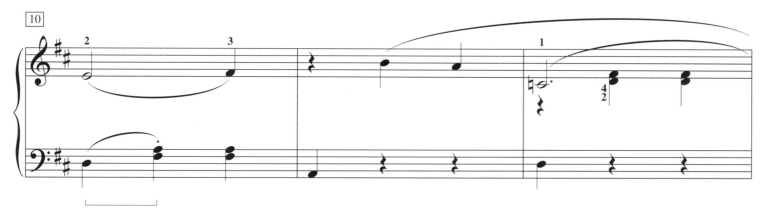

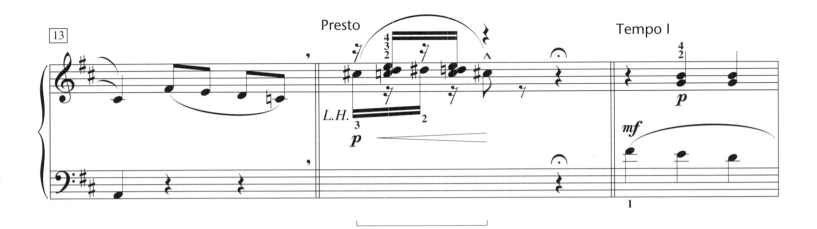

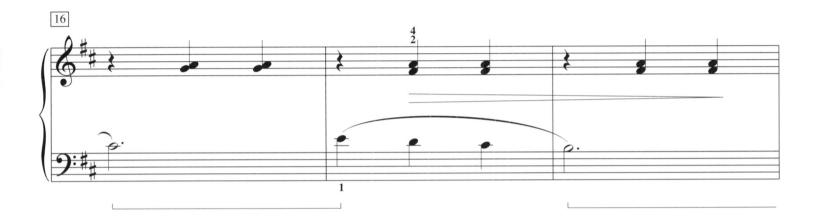

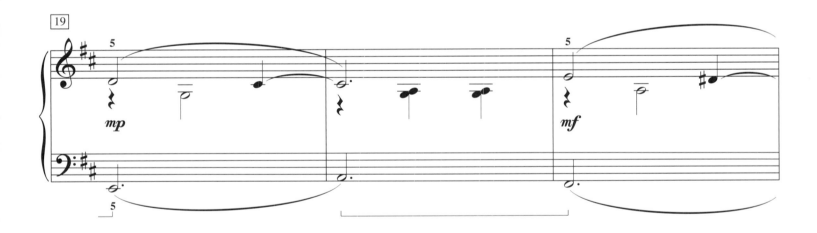

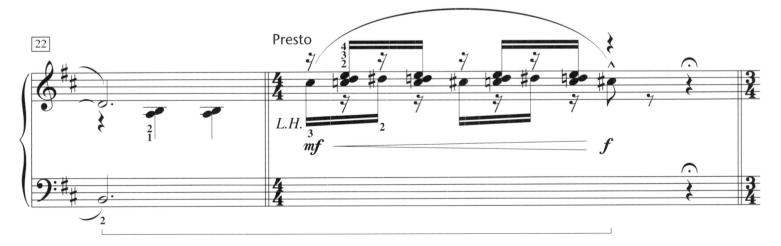

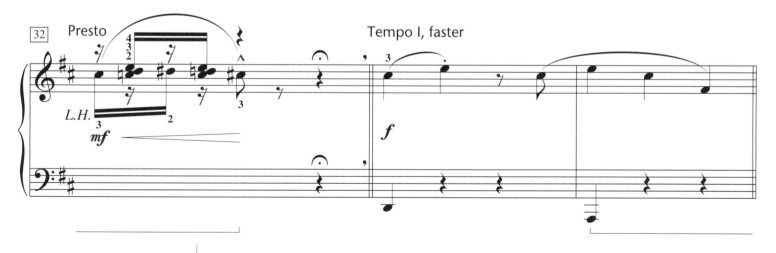

*Glissando for one beat. ✕ = approximate pitch.

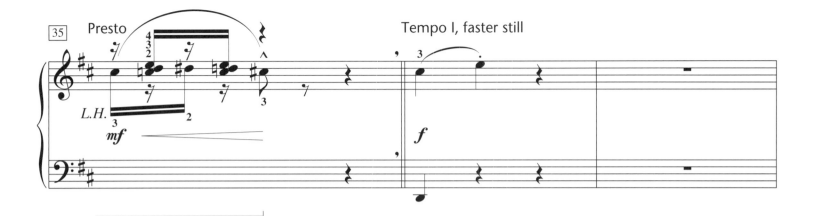

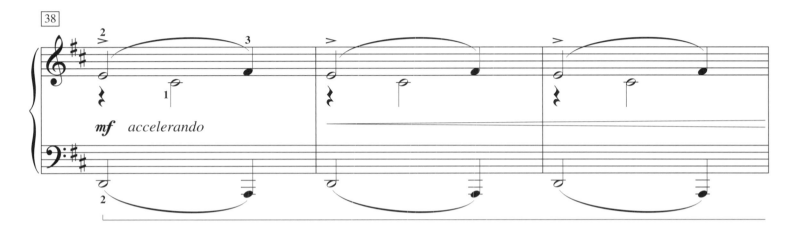

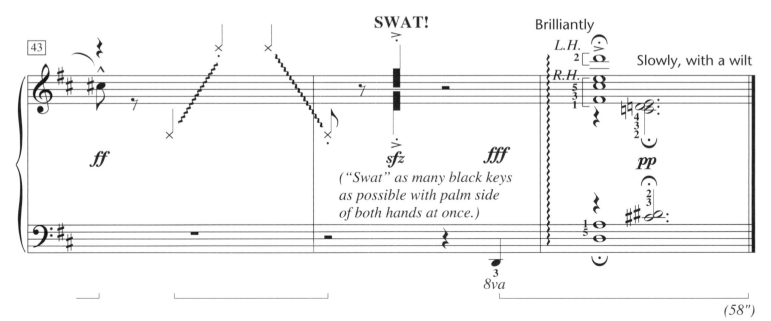

(58")

PERFORMANCE NOTES

The waltz has been popular since the late 1700s, making it the oldest of all ballroom dances. Its swirling character grew out of a lively 3/4 peasant dance for couples, which developed particularly in 18th-century Germany. Over the years, the waltz spread throughout Europe and became more refined and elegant, reaching its greatest popularity in the late 1800s with the music of composers like Johann Strauss, Jr., the "Waltz King."

While all waltzes are written in 3/4 or triple time, the music itself can portray a variety of styles and emotions. I hope you enjoy exploring the moods in these waltzes as much as I enjoyed dreaming them up.

–Carol Klose

Crystal Ballerina
(Music Box waltz)

This piece was inspired by one of my prized childhood possessions: a music box topped with a tiny mechanical crystal ballerina. I loved to wind the key, move the tiny lever to "start," and watch the fragile dancer spin round and round to a delicate waltz melody, until she gradually wound down to a gentle stop.

To recreate a music box dancer in this piece, keep the tempo very steady, until the *ritardando* in measure 32. From that point on, picture the ballerina slowing down gradually, as you bring the music to a complete stop at the end of the piece.

Focus on the R.H. melody, using less arm weight for the L.H. accompaniment, so that it stays at least one dynamic level softer than the R.H. In measures 33–37, however, use slightly more arm weight on the descending *tenuto* L.H. notes, using them to prepare for the *ritardando* that ends the piece. Be sure to hold down the damper pedal throughout those five measures.

In the R.H. part, look for repeated eighth-note patterns like those below.

measures 1–2

For a smooth *legato* flow in measures like these, play on the corner of your R.H. thumb, keeping a level wrist and allowing your arm to follow your hand. Group six eighth notes into "one" by playing the note on beat one with slightly more arm weight, followed by a *diminuendo* for the remaining five notes in the measure.

In measures 7, 23, 39, and 40, you will find an unusual combination: *staccato* notes along with the damper pedal. By playing these *staccatos* lightly and crisply with the damper pedal down, you can activate bell-like "pinging" sounds on the piano, adding to the music-box effect.

Transylvania Ball
(Macabre waltz)

This eerie waltz grew out of my childhood memories of scary Friday nights spent curled up on the sofa with my best friend, glued to the weekly Fright Night movie on TV while munching nervously on popcorn and salted sour apples. Our favorite flicks were the old vampire black-and-white movies, which took place in and around Count Dracula's dilapidated medieval castle in Transylvania.

If vampires were to hold a ball, perhaps they would waltz to music like this, stepping lightly in their black capes and flowing gowns to a sinister melody in C minor, with dramatic accents, shocking dynamic changes, and plenty of weird-sounding notes thrown in for good measure. As you learn this piece, try mapping out the dynamics so they do not take *you* by surprise.

The piece is in A/B/A1 form, with a coda (measures 53–59) that ushers in the sun's first rays, a vampire's signal to head back to the coffin. Play measures 56–59 very slowly, to get the most out of the surprise ending in E-flat major (the relative major of C minor). If you slowly sing "Good night" along with the music in measures 57 and 58, you'll get the tempo just right.

To play the eighth-note patterns smoothly in measures 1, 3, 5, etc., simply "hand" the notes from one hand to the other. Shape each group of eighth notes within a slur with a definite *crescendo* and *diminuendo*.

measures 1–2

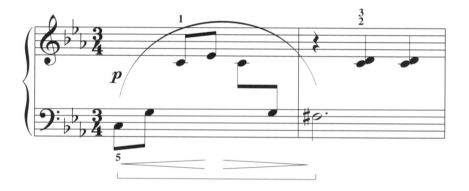

In measures 53–55, notice the change to 4/4. Simply continue counting the quarter-note pulse at the same tempo, but in "four," with a slight accent on beats one and three. Slow down gradually in those measures, to prepare for the long pause on beat three of measure 55, where 3/4 returns.

Lullaby in Blue
(Jazz waltz)

Many of the melodic and harmonic intervals in this tender waltz combine to form jazz sounds. As you learn this piece, listen especially for the colors produced by sevenths and seconds. Play the accompaniment intervals softly, blending them with careful pedaling, to surround the melody with subtle jazz harmonies.

Upstemmed and downstemmed notes that appear on the same staff (either treble or bass) indicate two or more voices played by the same hand. In this piece, upstemmed R.H. notes belong to the melody, while downstemmed R.H. notes are part of the accompaniment.

measures 1–2

Play the R.H. upstemmed dotted half notes with more arm weight, holding them for three full beats. Play the downstemmed accompaniment notes softly. Listen for the gentle rocking motion produced by R.H. two-note slurs that appear under the melody on beats two and three (for example, measures 1, 2, 4, 7, etc.).

Upstemmed and downstemmed notes also appear throughout the L.H. accompaniment. Use more arm weight for each downstemmed dotted half note on beat one, and lightly play the upstemmed half note on beat two.

measures 1–2

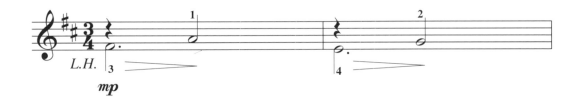

The ascending arpeggios in measures 33–37 are built mainly on the interval of a fourth. By holding down the damper pedal throughout those measures, you will create a beautiful blend of impressionistic jazz colors to end this gentle piece.

The final note, low D in measure 40, should imitate the sound of a plucked string bass. Be sure to play that D with a delicate *staccato* touch, releasing the damper pedal at the same time.

Petite Waltz
(Viennese waltz)

When playing this graceful piece, imagine elegant couples dressed in tuxedos and flowing satin gowns, swirling across the floor of a spacious gilt ballroom in 19th-century Austria. When you know the music well, let each measure fall into one beat, to recreate the feel of a lilting Viennese waltz.

The B section begins at measure 21. Notice the musical aspects that make it much more dramatic than the flowing A section:
- the change from the key of B-flat major to its relative minor, G minor
- *forte* dynamics
- no damper pedal
- a slightly faster tempo

Measures 36–48 form a transition that begins with abrupt *staccatos*, rests, and strong accents.

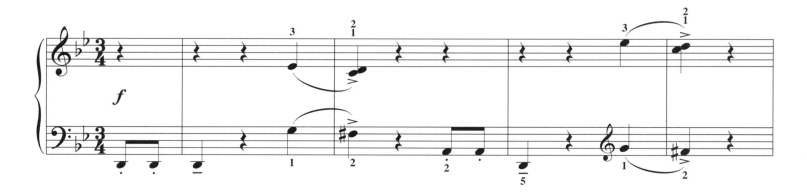

Think of those measures as a signal for the dancers to change partners. In measures 41–48 in this transition, imagine the dancers taking their new positions as the alternating seconds, descending five-note patterns, and *diminuendo* lead them back to the graceful, pleasant A section after the *da capo*.

The A section and Coda contain many eighth-note patterns that are repeated in different octaves. When you learn the following R.H. pattern in measure 1,

you will already know how to play measures 2, 3, 9, and 10.

Similarly, when you can play the following pattern in measure 17,

you will know measures 18, 51, 52, 53, and 54. In these measures, place your L.H. thumb over your right, so that your hands do not get tangled.

R.H. finger 5 begins each pattern. To move fast enough to play the next pattern on time, remember to play the last R.H. note lightly, as if dusting the key with your thumb. Use that dusting motion to shift your hand immediately to the next octave, so that finger 5 is ready to begin the next pattern.

Maestro, There's A Fly In My Waltz
(Scherzo waltz)

Have you ever experienced trying to play the piano with a pesky fly circling your head? In this scherzo, or "musical joke," use your imagination to create that fly, which has the audacity to interrupt this lovely D Major waltz. As the piece progresses, the fly becomes more and more annoying, until finally you will have no choice but to get rid of it with a big SWAT! The more you act out this story, the more fun you and your audience will have with the piece.

Practice the first "Fly motif" on its own:

measure 7

Then practice measures 7, 14, 23, 27–28, 32, 35, and 42–43, which contain repetitions or variations of this motif. Stay close to the keys, and imitate a buzzing sound by playing the sixteenth notes very fast. Place your L.H. on top of your R.H., playing with strong curved fingers as close to the keys as possible. Pedal exactly as shown, releasing the pedal as you strike the last note, which should be played with a strong, crisp accent.

Above the staff at the end of measures 13, 28, 32, and 35, observe the small comma, the sign to pause for a musical breath. Use this pause to shift gears as you return to the pleasant waltz melody.

All the musical events in the ending (measures 42–45) should happen very fast with a great deal of sound. They will be easier to play if you memorize the sequence of actions and practice them several times, saying to yourself:

Fly motif, *gliss* up, *gliss* down, SWAT, rest, low D (pedal), BIG chord (hold), soft "wilt" (hold)

Leave the damper pedal down throughout both *glissandi*, releasing it with the final note of the second *glissando*. With great energy, use your open palms to "swat" all the black keys you can in the middle of the keyboard. Immediately swing your L.H. down for the low D, catch the sound with the pedal, and quickly follow it with the *fff* arpeggiando chord in measure 45. Let the piano reverberate with as much sound as possible, playing from the bottom note of the chord to the top, crossing L.H. over for the high D. Take your time before you play the soft "wilt" chord at the end. It is no accident that that "dying" chord cluster is made up of all five notes of the "Fly motif." Have fun!